This planner belongs to

....

....

....

"A goal without a plan is just a wish"
Antoine de Saint-Exupery

January

S	M	T	W	T	F	S
			1	2	3	4
5	6	7	8	9	10	11
12	13	14	15	16	17	18
19	20	21	22	23	24	25
26	27	28	29	30	31	

February

S	M	T	W	T	F	S
						1
2	3	4	5	6	7	8
9	10	11	12	13	14	15
16	17	18	19	20	21	22
23	24	25	26	27	28	29

March

S	M	T	W	T	F	S
1	2	3	4	5	6	7
8	9	10	11	12	13	14
15	16	17	18	19	20	21
22	23	24	25	26	27	28
29	30	31				

April

S	M	T	W	T	F	S
			1	2	3	4
5	6	7	8	9	10	11
12	13	14	15	16	17	18
19	20	21	22	23	24	25
26	27	28	29	30		

May

S	M	T	W	T	F	S
					1	2
3	4	5	6	7	8	9
10	11	12	13	14	15	16
17	18	19	20	21	22	23
24	25	26	27	28	29	30
31						

June

S	M	T	W	T	F	S
	1	2	3	4	5	6
7	8	9	10	11	12	13
14	15	16	17	18	19	20
21	22	23	24	25	26	27
28	29	30				

July

S	M	T	W	T	F	S
			1	2	3	4
5	6	7	8	9	10	11
12	13	14	15	16	17	18
19	20	21	22	23	24	25
26	27	28	29	30	31	

August

S	M	T	W	T	F	S
						1
2	3	4	5	6	7	8
9	10	11	12	13	14	15
16	17	18	19	20	21	22
23	24	25	26	27	28	29
30	31					

September

S	M	T	W	T	F	S
		1	2	3	4	5
6	7	8	9	10	11	12
13	14	15	16	17	18	19
20	21	22	23	24	25	26
27	28	29	30			

October

S	M	T	W	T	F	S
				1	2	3
4	5	6	7	8	9	10
11	12	13	14	15	16	17
18	19	20	21	22	23	24
25	26	27	28	29	30	31

November

S	M	T	W	T	F	S
1	2	3	4	5	6	7
8	9	10	11	12	13	14
15	16	17	18	19	20	21
22	23	24	25	26	27	28
29	30					

December

S	M	T	W	T	F	S
		1	2	3	4	5
6	7	8	9	10	11	12
13	14	15	16	17	18	19
20	21	22	23	24	25	26
27	28	29	30	31		

Contacts

Name	Info

Passwords

Website _____ Website _____
User ID _____ User ID _____
Password _____ Password _____

Website _____ Website _____
User ID _____ User ID _____
Password _____ Password _____

Website _____ Website _____
User ID _____ User ID _____
Password _____ Password _____

Website _____ Website _____
User ID _____ User ID _____
Password _____ Password _____

Website _____ Website _____
User ID _____ User ID _____
Password _____ Password _____

Website _____ Website _____
User ID _____ User ID _____
Password _____ Password _____

Website _____ Website _____
User ID _____ User ID _____
Password _____ Password _____

Parties

Celebration	Info

How was my day?
(Mood Tracker)

	J	F	M	A	M	J	J	A	S	O	N	D
1												
2												
3												
4												
5												
6												
7												
8												
9												
10												
11												
12												
13												
14												
15												
16												
17												
18												
19												
20												
21												
22												
23												
24												
25												
26												
27												
28												
29												
30												
31												

- ☐ amazing, fantastic day
- ☐ really good, happy day
- ☐ normal, average day
- ☐ exhausted, tired day
- ☐ depressed, sad day
- ☐ frustrated, angry day
- ☐ stressed-out, frantic day

January

Sunday	Monday	Tuesday	Wednesday
29	30	31	1
5	6	7	8
12	13	14	15
19	20	21	22
26	27	28	29

"Health is the greatest gift, contentment the greatest wealth, faithfulness the best relationship" Buddha

2020

Thursday	Friday	Saturday
2	3	4
9	10	11
16	17	18
23	24	25
30	31	1

The Weekly Plan

Goals for the week

1.
2.
3.

To Do List

Schedule

Sun

Mon

Tue

Wed

Thu

Fri

Sat

Habits

	S	M	T	W	T	F	S

"Let all that you do be done in love" Corinthians 16:14

December 29 - January 4

Notes

1.
2.
3.

Meal Plan

Sun

Mon

Tue

Wed

Thu

Fri

Sat

Shopping List

-
-
-
-
-
-
-
-
-
-

Expenses

	S	M	T	W	T	F	S

The Weekly Plan

Goals for the week

1.
2.
3.

To Do List

Schedule

Sun

Mon

Tue

Wed

Thu

Fri

Sat

Habits

	S	M	T	W	T	F	S

"Noble deeds that are concealed are most esteemed" Blaise Pascal

January 5-11

Notes

1.
2.
3.

Shopping List

-
-
-
-
-
-
-
-
-

Meal Plan

Sun

Mon

Tue

Wed

Thu

Fri

Sat

Expenses

	S	M	T	W	T	F	S

The Weekly Plan

Goals for the week

1.
2.
3.

To Do List

-
-
-
-
-
-
-

Schedule

Sun

Mon

Tue

Wed

Thu

Fri

Sat

Habits

	S	M	T	W	T	F	S

"Live your beliefs and you can turn the world around" Henry David Thoreau

January 12-18

Notes

1.
2.
3.

Meal Plan

Sun

Mon

Tue

Wed

Thu

Fri

Sat

Shopping List

-
-
-
-
-
-
-
-
-
-

Expenses

	S	M	T	W	T	F	S

The Weekly Plan

Goals for the week

1.
2.
3.

To Do List

Schedule

Sun

Mon

Tue

Wed

Thu

Fri

Sat

Habits

	S	M	T	W	T	F	S

"Enthusiasm moves the world" Arthur Balfour

January 19-25

Notes

1.
2.
3.

Shopping List

-
-
-
-
-
-
-
-
-

Meal Plan

Sun	
Mon	
Tue	
Wed	
Thu	
Fri	
Sat	

Expenses

	S	M	T	W	T	F	S

The Weekly Plan

Goals for the week

1.
2.
3.

To Do List

-
-
-
-
-
-
-

Schedule

Sun

Mon

Tue

Wed

Thu

Fri

Sat

Habits

	S	M	T	W	T	F	S

"One today is worth two tomorrows" Benjamin Franklin

January 26 – February 1

Notes

1.
2.
3.

Meal Plan

Sun

Mon

Tue

Wed

Thu

Fri

Sat

Shopping List

-
-
-
-
-
-
-
-
-

Expenses

	S	M	T	W	T	F	S

February

Sunday	Monday	Tuesday	Wednesday
26	27	28	29
2	3	4	5
9	10	11	12
16	17	18	19
23	24	25	26

....
....
....
....
....
....
....
....
....

"Opportunities multiply as they are seized" Sun Tzu

2020

Thursday	Friday	Saturday
30	31	1
6	7	8
13	14	15
20	21	22
27	28	29

The Weekly Plan

Goals for the week

1.
2.
3.

To Do List

Schedule

Sun

Mon

Tue

Wed

Thu

Fri

Sat

Habits

	S	M	T	W	T	F	S

"To the mind that is still, the whole universe surrenders" Lao Tzu

February 2-8

Notes

1.
2.
3.

Shopping List

Meal Plan

Sun

Mon

Tue

Wed

Thu

Fri

Sat

Expenses

	S	M	T	W	T	F	S

The Weekly Plan

Goals for the week

1.
2.
3.

To Do List

Schedule

Sun

Mon

Tue

Wed

Thu

Fri

Sat

Habits

	S	M	T	W	T	F	S

"When deeds speak, words are nothing" Pierre-Joseph Proudhon

February 9-15

Notes

1.
2.
3.

Shopping List

-
-
-
-
-
-
-
-
-
-

Meal Plan

Sun

Mon

Tue

Wed

Thu

Fri

Sat

Expenses

	S	M	T	W	T	F	S

The Weekly Plan

Goals for the week

1.
2.
3.

Schedule

Sun

Mon

Tue

Wed

Thu

Fri

Sat

To Do List

Habits

	S	M	T	W	T	F	S

"I think; therefore I am" René Descartes

February 16-22

Notes

1.
2.
3.

Shopping List

-
-
-
-
-
-
-
-
-

Meal Plan

Sun

Mon

Tue

Wed

Thu

Fri

Sat

Expenses

	S	M	T	W	T	F	S

The Weekly Plan

Goals for the week

1.
2.
3.

To Do List

-
-
-
-
-
-
-

Schedule

Sun

Mon

Tue

Wed

Thu

Fri

Sat

Habits

	S	M	T	W	T	F	S

"No act of kindness, no matter how small, is ever wasted" Aesop

February 23-29

Notes

1.
2.
3.

Shopping List

-
-
-
-
-
-
-
-
-
-

Meal Plan

Sun

Mon

Tue

Wed

Thu

Fri

Sat

Expenses

	S	M	T	W	T	F	S

March

Sunday	Monday	Tuesday	Wednesday
1	2	3	4
8	9	10	11
15	16	17	18
22	23	24	25
29	30	31	

"What we think, we become" Buddha

2020

Thursday	Friday	Saturday
5	6	7
12	13	14
19	20	21
26	27	28
2	3	4

The Weekly Plan

Goals for the week

1.
2.
3.

Schedule

Sun

Mon

Tue

Wed

Thu

Fri

Sat

To Do List

Habits

	S	M	T	W	T	F	S

"It is during our darkest moments that we must focus to see the light" Aristotle

March 1-7

Notes

1.
2.
3.

Shopping List

Meal Plan

Sun

Mon

Tue

Wed

Thu

Fri

Sat

Expenses

	S	M	T	W	T	F	S

The Weekly Plan

Goals for the week

1.
2.
3.

Schedule

Sun

Mon

To Do List

-
-
-
-
-
-
-

Tue

Wed

Thu

Fri

Sat

Habits

	S	M	T	W	T	F	S

"Put your heart, mind, and soul into even your smallest acts. This is the secret of success" Swami Sivananda

March 8-14

Notes

1.
2.
3.

Shopping List

○
○
○
○
○
○
○
○
○

Meal Plan

Sun

Mon

Tue

Wed

Thu

Fri

Sat

Expenses

	S	M	T	W	T	F	S

The Weekly Plan

Goals for the week

1.
2.
3.

To Do List

-
-
-
-
-
-
-

Schedule

Sun

Mon

Tue

Wed

Thu

Fri

Sat

Habits

	S	M	T	W	T	F	S

"We know what we are, but know not what we may be" William Shakespeare

March 15-21

Notes

1.
2.
3.

Shopping List

-
-
-
-
-
-
-
-
-

Meal Plan

Sun

Mon

Tue

Wed

Thu

Fri

Sat

Expenses

	S	M	T	W	T	F	S

The Weekly Plan

Goals for the week

1.
2.
3.

To Do List

Schedule

Sun

Mon

Tue

Wed

Thu

Fri

Sat

Habits

	S	M	T	W	T	F	S

"Wealth is the product of man's capacity to think" Ayn Rand

March 22-28

Notes

1.
2.
3.

Shopping List

-
-
-
-
-
-
-
-
-

Meal Plan

Sun

Mon

Tue

Wed

Thu

Fri

Sat

Expenses

	S	M	T	W	T	F	S

The Weekly Plan

Goals for the week

1.
2.
3.

Schedule

Sun

Mon

Tue

Wed

Thu

Fri

Sat

To Do List

Habits

	S	M	T	W	T	F	S

"Keep your face always toward the sunshine - and shadows will fall behind you" Walt Whitman

March 29 - April 4

Notes

1.
2.
3.

Shopping List

-
-
-
-
-
-
-
-
-

Meal Plan

Sun

Mon

Tue

Wed

Thu

Fri

Sat

Expenses

	S	M	T	W	T	F	S

April

Sunday	Monday	Tuesday	Wednesday
29	30	31	1
5	6	7	8
12	13	14	15
19	20	21	22
26	27	28	29

"Never was anything great achieved without danger" Niccolò Machiavelli

2020

Thursday	Friday	Saturday
2	3	4
9	10	11
16	17	18
23	24	25
30	1	2

The Weekly Plan

Goals for the week

1.
2.
3.

To Do List

Schedule

Sun

Mon

Tue

Wed

Thu

Fri

Sat

Habits

	S	M	T	W	T	F	S

"Beauty in things exists in the mind which contemplates them" David Hume

April 5-11

Notes

1.
2.
3.

Shopping List

-
-
-
-
-
-
-
-
-

Meal Plan

Sun

Mon

Tue

Wed

Thu

Fri

Sat

Expenses

	S	M	T	W	T	F	S

The Weekly Plan

Goals for the week

1.
2.
3.

To Do List

Schedule

Sun

Mon

Tue

Wed

Thu

Fri

Sat

Habits

	S	M	T	W	T	F	S

"Science is organized knowledge. Wisdom is organized life" Immanuel Kant

April 12-18

Notes

1.
2.
3.

Shopping List

-
-
-
-
-
-
-
-

Meal Plan

Sun

Mon

Tue

Wed

Thu

Fri

Sat

Expenses

	S	M	T	W	T	F	S

The Weekly Plan

Goals for the week

1.
2.
3.

To Do List

-
-
-
-
-
-
-

Schedule

Sun

Mon

Tue

Wed

Thu

Fri

Sat

Habits

	S	M	T	W	T	F	S

"What worries you, masters you" — John Locke

April 19-25

Notes

1.
2.
3.

Shopping List

-
-
-
-
-
-
-
-
-

Meal Plan

Sun

Mon

Tue

Wed

Thu

Fri

Sat

Expenses

	S	M	T	W	T	F	S

The Weekly Plan

Goals for the week

1.
2.
3.

To Do List

-
-
-
-
-
-
-

Schedule

Sun

Mon

Tue

Wed

Thu

Fri

Sat

Habits

	S	M	T	W	T	F	S

"The things that we love tell us what we are" Thomas Aquinas

April 26 - May 2

Notes

1.
2.
3.

Shopping List

-
-
-
-
-
-
-
-
-
-

Meal Plan

Sun

Mon

Tue

Wed

Thu

Fri

Sat

Expenses

	S	M	T	W	T	F	S

May

Sunday	Monday	Tuesday	Wednesday
26	27	28	29
3	4	5	6
10	11	12	13
17	18	19	20
24	25	26	27

....
....
....
....
....
....
....
....

"I want you to be everything that's you, deep at the center of your being" Confucius

2020

Thursday	Friday	Saturday
30	1	2
7	8	9
14	15	16
21	22	23
28	29	30/31

The Weekly Plan

Goals for the week

1.
2.
3.

To Do List

Schedule

Sun

Mon

Tue

Wed

Thu

Fri

Sat

Habits

	S	M	T	W	T	F	S

"In the middle of difficulty lies opportunity" Albert Einstein

May 3-9

Notes

1.
2.
3.

Shopping List

-
-
-
-
-
-
-
-
-

Meal Plan

Sun

Mon

Tue

Wed

Thu

Fri

Sat

Expenses

	S	M	T	W	T	F	S

The Weekly Plan

Goals for the week

1.
2.
3.

To Do List

-
-
-
-
-
-
-

Schedule

Sun

Mon

Tue

Wed

Thu

Fri

Sat

Habits

	S	M	T	W	T	F	S

"He who believes is strong; he who doubts is weak. Strong convictions precede great actions" Louisa May Alcott

May 10-16

Notes

1.
2.
3.

Shopping List

-
-
-
-
-
-
-
-
-

Meal Plan

Sun

Mon

Tue

Wed

Thu

Fri

Sat

Expenses

	S	M	T	W	T	F	S

The Weekly Plan

Goals for the week

1.
2.
3.

To Do List

Schedule

Sun

Mon

Tue

Wed

Thu

Fri

Sat

Habits

	S	M	T	W	T	F	S

"All that glitters is not gold" William Shakespeare

May 17-23

Notes

1.
2.
3.

Shopping List

-
-
-
-
-
-
-
-
-
-

Meal Plan

Sun

Mon

Tue

Wed

Thu

Fri

Sat

Expenses

	S	M	T	W	T	F	S

The Weekly Plan

Goals for the week

1.
2.
3.

To Do List

-
-
-
-
-
-
-

Schedule

Sun

Mon

Tue

Wed

Thu

Fri

Sat

Habits

	S	M	T	W	T	F	S

"The power of imagination makes us infinite" John Muir

May 24-30

Notes

1.
2.
3.

Shopping List

-
-
-
-
-
-
-
-
-

Meal Plan

Sun

Mon

Tue

Wed

Thu

Fri

Sat

Expenses

	S	M	T	W	T	F	S

June

Sunday	Monday	Tuesday	Wednesday
31	1	2	3
7	8	9	10
14	15	16	17
21	22	23	24
28	29	30	1

"No great discovery was ever made without a bold guess" Isaac Newton

2020

Thursday	Friday	Saturday
4	5	6
11	12	13
18	19	20
25	26	27
2	3	4

The Weekly Plan

Goals for the week

1.
2.
3.

To Do List

Schedule

Sun

Mon

Tue

Wed

Thu

Fri

Sat

Habits

	S	M	T	W	T	F	S

"Thinking: the talking of the soul with itself" Plato

May 31 - June 6

Notes

1.
2.
3.

Shopping List

Meal Plan

Sun

Mon

Tue

Wed

Thu

Fri

Sat

Expenses

	S	M	T	W	T	F	S

The Weekly Plan

Goals for the week

1.
2.
3.

To Do List

-
-
-
-
-
-
-

Schedule

Sun

Mon

Tue

Wed

Thu

Fri

Sat

Habits

	S	M	T	W	T	F	S

"Give light, and the darkness will disappear of itself" Desiderius Erasmus

June 7-13

Notes

1.
2.
3.

Shopping List

Meal Plan

Sun

Mon

Tue

Wed

Thu

Fri

Sat

Expenses

	S	M	T	W	T	F	S

The Weekly Plan

Goals for the week

1.
2.
3.

To Do List

-
-
-
-
-
-
-

Schedule

Sun

Mon

Tue

Wed

Thu

Fri

Sat

Habits

	S	M	T	W	T	F	S

"The course of true love never did run smooth" William Shakespeare

June 14-20

Notes

1.
2.
3.

Shopping List

Meal Plan

Sun

Mon

Tue

Wed

Thu

Fri

Sat

Expenses

	S	M	T	W	T	F	S

The Weekly Plan

Goals for the week

1.
2.
3.

To Do List

Schedule

Sun

Mon

Tue

Wed

Thu

Fri

Sat

Habits

	S	M	T	W	T	F	S

"The question isn't who is going to let me; it's who is going to stop me" Ayn Rand

June 21-27

Notes

1.
2.
3.

Shopping List

-
-
-
-
-
-
-
-
-
-

Meal Plan

Sun

Mon

Tue

Wed

Thu

Fri

Sat

Expenses

	S	M	T	W	T	F	S

The Weekly Plan

Goals for the week

1.
2.
3.

To Do List

Schedule

Sun

Mon

Tue

Wed

Thu

Fri

Sat

Habits

	S	M	T	W	T	F	S

"The question isn't who is going to let me; it's who is going to stop me" Ayn Rand

June 28 - July 4

Notes

1.
2.
3.

Shopping List

-
-
-
-
-
-
-
-
-

Meal Plan

Sun

Mon

Tue

Wed

Thu

Fri

Sat

Expenses

S	M	T	W	T	F	S

July

Sunday	Monday	Tuesday	Wednesday
28	29	30	1
5	6	7	8
12	13	14	15
19	20	21	22
26	27	28	29

....
....
....
....
....
....
....
....

"I hear and I forget. I see and I remember. I do and I understand" Confucius

2020

Thursday	Friday	Saturday
2	3	4
9	10	11
16	17	18
23	24	25
30	31	1

The Weekly Plan

Goals for the week

1.
2.
3.

To Do List

-
-
-
-
-
-
-

Schedule

Sun

Mon

Tue

Wed

Thu

Fri

Sat

Habits

	S	M	T	W	T	F	S

"Difficulties are meant to rouse, not discourage. The human spirit is to grow strong by conflic" William Ellery

July 5-11

Notes

1.
2.
3.

Shopping List

Meal Plan

Sun

Mon

Tue

Wed

Thu

Fri

Sat

Expenses

S	M	T	W	T	F	S

The Weekly Plan

Goals for the week

1.
2.
3.

To Do List

-
-
-
-
-
-
-

Schedule

Sun

Mon

Tue

Wed

Thu

Fri

Sat

Habits

	S	M	T	W	T	F	S

"Nothing can harm you as much as your own thoughts unguarded" Buddha

July 12-18

Notes

1.
2.
3.

Shopping List

-
-
-
-
-
-
-
-
-
-

Meal Plan

Sun

Mon

Tue

Wed

Thu

Fri

Sat

Expenses

	S	M	T	W	T	F	S

The Weekly Plan

Goals for the week

1.
2.
3.

To Do List

-
-
-
-
-
-
-

Schedule

Sun

Mon

Tue

Wed

Thu

Fri

Sat

Habits

	S	M	T	W	T	F	S

"There is nothing impossible to him who will try" Alexander the Great

July 19-25

Notes

1.
2.
3.

Shopping List

-
-
-
-
-
-
-
-
-
-

Meal Plan

Sun

Mon

Tue

Wed

Thu

Fri

Sat

Expenses

	S	M	T	W	T	F	S

The Weekly Plan

Goals for the week

1.
2.
3.

To Do List

-
-
-
-
-
-
-

Schedule

Sun

Mon

Tue

Wed

Thu

Fri

Sat

Habits

	S	M	T	W	T	F	S

"Noble deeds that are concealed are most esteemed" Blaise Pascal

July 26 - August 1

Notes

1.
2.
3.

Shopping List

-
-
-
-
-
-
-
-
-

Meal Plan

Sun

Mon

Tue

Wed

Thu

Fri

Sat

Expenses

	S	M	T	W	T	F	S

August

Sunday	Monday	Tuesday	Wednesday
26	27	28	29
2	3	4	5
9	10	11	12
16	17	18	19
23	24	25	26

"It is not enough to have a good mind; the main thing is to use it well" René Descartes

2020

Thursday	Friday	Saturday
30	31	1
6	7	8
13	14	15
20	21	22
27	28	29

The Weekly Plan

Goals for the week

1.
2.
3.

To Do List

-
-
-
-
-
-
-

Schedule

Sun

Mon

Tue

Wed

Thu

Fri

Sat

Habits

	S	M	T	W	T	F	S

"The things that we love tell us what we are" Thomas Aquinas

August 2-8

Notes

1.
2.
3.

Shopping List

○
○
○
○
○
○
○
○
○

Meal Plan

Sun

Mon

Tue

Wed

Thu

Fri

Sat

Expenses

	S	M	T	W	T	F	S

The Weekly Plan

Goals for the week

1.
2.
3.

To Do List

-
-
-
-
-
-

Schedule

Sun

Mon

Tue

Wed

Thu

Fri

Sat

Habits

	S	M	T	W	T	F	S

"Know your enemy and know yourself and you can fight a hundred battles without disaster" Sun Tzu

August 9-15

Notes

1.
2.
3.

Shopping List

Meal Plan

Sun

Mon

Tue

Wed

Thu

Fri

Sat

Expenses

	S	M	T	W	T	F	S

The Weekly Plan

Goals for the week

1.
2.
3.

To Do List

-
-
-
-
-
-
-

Schedule

Sun

Mon

Tue

Wed

Thu

Fri

Sat

Habits

	S	M	T	W	T	F	S

"The whole is more than the sum of its parts" Aristotle

August 16-22

Notes

1.
2.
3.

Shopping List

-
-
-
-
-
-
-
-
-
-

Meal Plan

Sun

Mon

Tue

Wed

Thu

Fri

Sat

Expenses

	S	M	T	W	T	F	S

The Weekly Plan

Goals for the week

1.
2.
3.

To Do List

-
-
-
-
-
-
-

Schedule

Sun

Mon

Tue

Wed

Thu

Fri

Sat

Habits

	S	M	T	W	T	F	S

"Out of difficulties grow miracles" Jean de la Bruyere

August 23-29

Notes

1.
2.
3.

Shopping List

-
-
-
-
-
-
-
-
-
-

Meal Plan

Sun

Mon

Tue

Wed

Thu

Fri

Sat

Expenses

	S	M	T	W	T	F	S

The Weekly Plan

Goals for the week

1.
2.
3.

To Do List

Schedule

Sun

Mon

Tue

Wed

Thu

Fri

Sat

Habits

	S	M	T	W	T	F	S

"Love takes up where knowledge leaves off" Thomas Aquinas

August 30 - september 5

Notes

1.
2.
3.

Meal Plan

Sun	
Mon	
Tue	
Wed	
Thu	
Fri	
Sat	

Shopping List

-
-
-
-
-
-
-
-
-
-

Expenses

	S	M	T	W	T	F	S

September

Sunday	Monday	Tuesday	Wednesday
30	31	1	2
6	7	8	9
13	14	15	16
20	21	22	23
27	28	29	30

"Strength and growth come only through continuous effort and struggle" Napoleon Hill

2020

Thursday	Friday	Saturday
3	4	5
10	11	12
17	18	19
24	25	26
1	2	3

The Weekly Plan

Goals for the week

1.
2.
3.

Schedule

Sun

Mon

Tue

Wed

Thu

Fri

Sat

To Do List

-
-
-
-
-
-
-

Habits

	S	M	T	W	T	F	S

"When I let go of what I am, I become what I might be" Laozi

September 6-12

Notes

1.
2.
3.

Shopping List

-
-
-
-
-
-
-
-

Meal Plan

Sun

Mon

Tue

Wed

Thu

Fri

Sat

Expenses

	S	M	T	W	T	F	S

The Weekly Plan

Goals for the week

1.
2.
3.

To Do List

-
-
-
-
-
-
-

Schedule

Sun

Mon

Tue

Wed

Thu

Fri

Sat

Habits

	S	M	T	W	T	F	S

"From a small seed a mighty trunk may grow" Aeschylus

September 13-19

Notes

1.
2.
3.

Shopping List

-
-
-
-
-
-
-
-
-

Meal Plan

Sun

Mon

Tue

Wed

Thu

Fri

Sat

Expenses

	S	M	T	W	T	F	S

The Weekly Plan

Goals for the week

1.
2.
3.

To Do List

Schedule

Sun

Mon

Tue

Wed

Thu

Fri

Sat

Habits

	S	M	T	W	T	F	S

"Look within. Within is the fountain of good, and it will ever bubble up, if thou wilt ever dig" Marcus Aurelius

September 20-26

Notes

1.
2.
3.

Shopping List

Meal Plan

Sun

Mon

Tue

Wed

Thu

Fri

Sat

Expenses

	S	M	T	W	T	F	S

The Weekly Plan

Goals for the week

1.
2.
3.

To Do List

Schedule

Sun

Mon

Tue

Wed

Thu

Fri

Sat

Habits

	S	M	T	W	T	F	S

"If you truly loved yourself, you could never hurt another" Buddha

September 27 - october 3

Notes

1.
2.
3.

Shopping List

-
-
-
-
-
-
-
-
-

Meal Plan

Sun

Mon

Tue

Wed

Thu

Fri

Sat

Expenses

	S	M	T	W	T	F	S

October

Sunday	Monday	Tuesday	Wednesday
27	28	29	30
4	5	6	7
11	12	13	14
18	19	20	21
25	26	27	28

....
....
....
....
....
....
....
....
....

"Live your beliefs and you can turn the world around" Henry David Thoreau

2020

Thursday	Friday	Saturday
1	2	3
8	9	10
15	16	17
22	23	24
29	30	31

The Weekly Plan

Goals for the week

1.
2.
3.

To Do List

-
-
-
-
-
-
-

Schedule

Sun

Mon

Tue

Wed

Thu

Fri

Sat

Habits

	S	M	T	W	T	F	S

"Grace is the beauty of form under the influence of freedom" Friedrich Schiller

October 4-10

Notes

1.
2.
3.

Shopping List

Meal Plan

Sun

Mon

Tue

Wed

Thu

Fri

Sat

Expenses

	S	M	T	W	T	F	S

The Weekly Plan

Goals for the week

1.
2.
3.

To Do List

Schedule

Sun

Mon

Tue

Wed

Thu

Fri

Sat

Habits

	S	M	T	W	T	F	S

"There is nothing on this earth more to be prized than true friendship" Thomas Aquinas

October 11-17

Notes

1.
2.
3.

Meal Plan

Sun

Mon

Tue

Wed

Thu

Fri

Sat

Shopping List

-
-
-
-
-
-
-
-
-

Expenses

	S	M	T	W	T	F	S

The Weekly Plan

Goals for the week

1.
2.
3.

To Do List

-
-
-
-
-
-
-

Schedule

Sun

Mon

Tue

Wed

Thu

Fri

Sat

Habits

	S	M	T	W	T	F	S

"Every man's life is a fairy tale written by God's fingers" Hans Christian Andersen

October 18-24

Notes

1.
2.
3.

Shopping List

-
-
-
-
-
-
-
-
-
-

Meal Plan

Sun

Mon

Tue

Wed

Thu

Fri

Sat

Expenses

	S	M	T	W	T	F	S

The Weekly Plan

Goals for the week

1.
2.
3.

To Do List

-
-
-
-
-
-
-

Schedule

Sun

Mon

Tue

Wed

Thu

Fri

Sat

Habits

	S	M	T	W	T	F	S

"The only journey is the one within" Rainer Maria Rilke

October 21-31

Notes

1.
2.
3.

Shopping List

-
-
-
-
-
-
-
-
-

Meal Plan

| Sun |
| Mon |
| Tue |
| Wed |
| Thu |
| Fri |
| Sat |

Expenses

	S	M	T	W	T	F	S

November

Sunday	Monday	Tuesday	Wednesday
1	2	3	4
8	9	10	11
15	16	17	18
22	23	24	25
29	30	1	2

....
....
....
....
....
....
....
....
....

"Enthusiasm moves the world" Arthur Balfour

2020

Thursday	Friday	Saturday
5	6	7
12	13	14
19	20	21
26	27	28
3	4	5

The Weekly Plan

Goals for the week

1.
2.
3.

To Do List

-
-
-
-
-
-
-

Schedule

Sun

Mon

Tue

Wed

Thu

Fri

Sat

Habits

	S	M	T	W	T	F	S

"What makes the desert beautiful is that somewhere it hides a well" Antoine de Saint-Exupery

November 1-7

Notes

1.
2.
3.

Shopping List

-
-
-
-
-
-
-
-
-
-

Meal Plan

Sun

Mon

Tue

Wed

Thu

Fri

Sat

Expenses

	S	M	T	W	T	F	S

The Weekly Plan

Goals for the week

1.
2.
3.

To Do List

Schedule

Sun

Mon

Tue

Wed

Thu

Fri

Sat

Habits

	S	M	T	W	T	F	S

"It is beyond a doubt that all our knowledge that begins with experience" Immanuel Kant

November 8-14

Notes

1.
2.
3.

Shopping List

-
-
-
-
-
-
-
-
-
-

Meal Plan

| Sun |
| Mon |
| Tue |
| Wed |
| Thu |
| Fri |
| Sat |

Expenses

	S	M	T	W	T	F	S

The Weekly Plan

Goals for the week

1.
2.
3.

To Do List

-
-
-
-
-
-
-

Schedule

Sun

Mon

Tue

Wed

Thu

Fri

Sat

Habits

	S	M	T	W	T	F	S

"To the mind that is still, the whole universe surrenders" Lao Tzu

November 15-21

Notes

1.
2.
3.

Shopping List

Meal Plan

Sun

Mon

Tue

Wed

Thu

Fri

Sat

Expenses

	S	M	T	W	T	F	S

The Weekly Plan

Goals for the week

1.
2.
3.

To Do List

-
-
-
-
-
-
-

Schedule

Sun

Mon

Tue

Wed

Thu

Fri

Sat

Habits

	S	M	T	W	T	F	S

"A wise man proportions his belief to the evidence" David Hume

November 22-28

Notes

1.
2.
3.

Shopping List

-
-
-
-
-
-
-
-
-

Meal Plan

Sun	
Mon	
Tue	
Wed	
Thu	
Fri	
Sat	

Expenses

	S	M	T	W	T	F	S

The Weekly Plan

Goals for the week

1.
2.
3.

To Do List

-
-
-
-
-
-
-

Schedule

Sun

Mon

Tue

Wed

Thu

Fri

Sat

Habits

	S	M	T	W	T	F	S

"When deeds speak, words are nothing" Pierre-Joseph Proudhon

November 29 - december 5

Notes

1.
2.
3.

Shopping List

-
-
-
-
-
-
-
-
-
-

Meal Plan

Sun

Mon

Tue

Wed

Thu

Fri

Sat

Expenses

	S	M	T	W	T	F	S

December

Sunday	Monday	Tuesday	Wednesday
29	30	1	2
6	7	8	9
13	14	15	16
20	21	22	23
27	28	29	30

"The reading of all good books is like a conversation with the finest minds of past centuries" René Descartes

2020

Thursday	Friday	Saturday
3	4	5
10	11	12
17	18	19
24	25	26
31	1	2

The Weekly Plan

Goals for the week

1.
2.
3.

To Do List

-
-
-
-
-
-
-

Schedule

Sun

Mon

Tue

Wed

Thu

Fri

Sat

Habits

	S	M	T	W	T	F	S

"No act of kindness, no matter how small, is ever wasted" Aesop

December 6-12

Notes

1.
2.
3.

Meal Plan

Sun

Mon

Tue

Wed

Thu

Fri

Sat

Shopping List

Expenses

	S	M	T	W	T	F	S

The Weekly Plan

Goals for the week

1.
2.
3.

To Do List

-
-
-
-
-
-
-

Schedule

Sun

Mon

Tue

Wed

Thu

Fri

Sat

Habits

	S	M	T	W	T	F	S

"It is during our darkest moments that we must focus to see the light" Aristotle

December 13-19

Notes

1.
2.
3.

Shopping List

-
-
-
-
-
-
-
-
-

Meal Plan

Sun

Mon

Tue

Wed

Thu

Fri

Sat

Expenses

	S	M	T	W	T	F	S

The Weekly Plan

Goals for the week

1.
2.
3.

To Do List

Schedule

Sun

Mon

Tue

Wed

Thu

Fri

Sat

Habits

	S	M	T	W	T	F	S

"I cannot teach anybody anything, I can only make them think" Socrates

December 20-26

Notes

1.
2.
3.

Shopping List

-
-
-
-
-
-
-
-
-
-

Meal Plan

Sun

Mon

Tue

Wed

Thu

Fri

Sat

Expenses

	S	M	T	W	T	F	S

The Weekly Plan

Goals for the week

1.
2.
3.

To Do List

-
-
-
-
-
-
-

Schedule

Sun

Mon

Tue

Wed

Thu

Fri

Sat

Habits

	S	M	T	W	T	F	S

"Since love grows within you, so beauty grows. For love is the beauty of the soul" Augustinus

December 27 – January 2

Notes

1.
2.
3.

Meal Plan

Sun

Mon

Tue

Wed

Thu

Fri

Sat

Shopping List

-
-
-
-
-
-
-
-
-
-

Expenses

	S	M	T	W	T	F	S

The Weekly Plan

Goals for the week

1.
2.
3.

To Do List

Schedule

Sun

Mon

Tue

Wed

Thu

Fri

Sat

Habits

	S	M	T	W	T	F	S

"Judge of a man by his questions rather than by his answers" Voltaire

January 3-9

Notes

1.
2.
3.

Shopping List

-
-
-
-
-
-
-
-
-
-

Meal Plan

Sun

Mon

Tue

Wed

Thu

Fri

Sat

Expenses

	S	M	T	W	T	F	S

Notes

What MOVIE should I watch?

title	date watched	rating/comments

Notes

Books to Read

Notes

SAVING GOALS

December
November
October
September
August
July
June
May
April
March
February
January

Goal for each month is $........

Notes

Printed by Amazon Italia Logistica S.r.l.
Torrazza Piemonte (TO), Italy